Walter Crane

The sirens three

A poem

Walter Crane

The sirens three
A poem

ISBN/EAN: 9783742836564

Manufactured in Europe, USA, Canada, Australia, Japa

Cover: Foto ©Andreas Hilbeck / pixelio.de

Manufactured and distributed by brebook publishing software
(www.brebook.com)

Walter Crane

The sirens three

THE ~~~~~~~

IRENS THREE.

A POEM:

WRITTEN AND ILLUSTRATED
BY

WALTER · CRANE

:LONDON:
MACMILLAN & CO:
MDCCCLXXXVI:

TO WILLIAM MORRIS.

The Mage of Naishápúr in English tongue [1]
Beside the northern sea I, wandering, read;
With chaunt of breaking waves each verse was said,
Till, storm-possessed, my heart in answer sung;
And to the winds my ship of thoughts I flung,
And drifted wide upon the ocean dread
Of space and time, ere thought of life were bred,
Till Hope did cast the anchor, and I clung.

The book of Omar saw I, limned in gold,
And decked with vine and rose and pictured pause,
Enwrought by hands of one well-skilled and bold
In art of poesy and Freedom's cause,
Hope of humanity and equal laws:
To him and to this hope be mine enscrolled.

WALTER CRANE.

September, 1885.

[1] Rubáiyát of Omar Khayyám. Translated by Edward Fitzgerald.

The Sirens Three.

I.

LOST on a sleepless sea, without avail
My soul's ship drifted wide, with idle sail
And slow pulsating oars, that night's blue gulf
Beat noiselessly to Time's recurring tale.

II.

The rolling hours like waves broke, one by one,
Upon the tide of thought time's sands outrun,
And cloudy visions hovered o'er my bed,
Piled to the stars, full soon like cloud undone:

III.

As, like the wan moon through her fleecy sea,
My spirit clove their rack unceasingly,
And struck at last upon an unknown ground,
More still than sleep, more strange than dreamlands be.

IV.

The echoes of lost thoughts wild music made,
Like Sirens, heard above the winds that played,
Above the rythmic waves' tumultuous tone,
Upon the hollows of that coast decayed.

The Sirens Three.

V.

Yea, on the strand they stood, the Sirens three—
No More, and golden Now, and dark To Be,
Whose vocal harps are love, and hope, and grief;
To these they sang, and waved their hands to me.

VI.

Who thence, unto the shore, escaping, clung,
As from the dread insatiate ocean's tongue
That lapped the barren sand, and evermore,
Above its vain recoil, the Sisters sung.

VII.

Prone on that unknown land, outcast, forlorn,
My soul lay; watching for the eyes of morn;
As from a dying universe adrift,
A naked life—to what dim world new born?

VIII.

All former things had passed, the sea's salt tears
From Youth's frail ship had washed false hopes and fears,
And relics, treasured once, bestrewed the sand,
Wrapped in the clinging weed the seamaid wears.

IX.

The bodies of lost Faith and Love, outcast,
Spurned by the waves, and clinging to the mast,
Were flung upon the shore, mid drift and wreck,—
Time's fragile shells, which frailer lives outlast.

The Sirens Three.

X.

As at the world's end left, the last of men,
Or ere the first was sphered, beyond his ken,
Was I, mid tumbled kosmic fragments cast—
A babe at play within a mammoth's den :

XI.

Mid bones of power extinct, and its lost prey,
With shreds and shards of unknown primal day—
The formless Future, and the Past forgot,
The broken statue, and the sculptor's clay.

XII.

The blue-breast bird of space his fan outspread,
And shook the starry splendour o'er my head—
A wood of eyes that wonder at the world,
Glassed in the world's eyes' wonder, scanned and read :

XIII.

Each burning orb that did the sky emblaze
Upon my spirit lone cast piercing gaze ;
World beyond world enringed, and suns aflame
Shot from night's spangled cloud their storm of rays.

XIV.

As doth the glass to one bright point intense
Draw the sun's fervour to our shrinking sense ;
So, on my soul, the concentrated fire
Of countless suns that moment did condense.

XV.

My brain, an instant's Atlas, seemed to bear
The Universe immense, and all its care ;
For Thought's frail arms intolerable weight,
Since Nature's triumph still is Man's despair.

3

XVI.

Untilled, unknown, the trackless regions spread
Which Thought, belated wanderer, doth tread,
Where, like a river flashing through the night,
The milky way its myriad star-foam shed.

XVII.

Cast from what vital source—what teeming brain?
By blind persistent force—from fiery rain—
Suns, moons, and stars, transmuted, globed, and hung
The dew of Space upon its blue campaign :

XVIII.

Trod by the feet of Time, as he doth go,
A labourer night and morn to reap and sow—
Who counts them as they fall, or wonders well
If one should break with all his weight of woe?

XIX.

Each drop a desert, or a battle-ground
Of life in its arena ringed around,
Where without quarter wears the endless war,
Till Death the hunter slips his famished hound.

XX.

Here, circling with the horses of the sun,
Man's fateful race from day to day is run ;
Bound in this narrow ring—his crown, his grave—
Still as the world for each is lost or won.

XXI.

Then, like a homeless one, my spirit turned
For shelter 'neath the roofless void, and, spurned
From the star-desert to the stony one,
Scanned the dark waste where yet no hearth-fire burned:

XXII.

But through the veil of night, around me there,
Rose towering shapes clothed in the voiceless air,
Like kings enthroned amid their powers' decay—
Statue, and ruined shrine, and temple bare:

XXIII.

Dolmen, and sphinx, and Greek or Gothic fane,
The shattered caskets of man's winged brain,
Whose flight hath left them empty, desolate,
Sublime in ruin on the crumbling plain.

XXIV.

The perished bodies frail that once did house
His restless soul, and heard his sacred vows
To his own likeness, dressed in speech or stone,
Ere he forswore them for some fairer spouse.

XXV.

He sought for Truth, and cried, "Where dost thou dwell?"
Ten thousand tongues replied, but none could tell:
They held their peace, and then the stones did cry—
"Lo! Truth sits naked by the wayside well."

XXVI.

She sitteth naked since they drove her out
From Babel of the Creeds to wastes of Doubt;
There hath she wandered long in dens and caves,
Through Custom's winter, and through Reason's drought.

5

XXVII.

They would have cloaked her as a shameful thing;
Force brought her chains, and Fraud a marriage ring,
But Truth, afrighted, fled the market place
Where lies were coined in gold, and Craft was king.

XXVIII.

And still she flies from sacred fount, and school,
When man defiles, or doth his kind befool;
And still they wait, the halt, the lame, the blind,
Though Truth, the angel, troubleth not the pool.

XXIX.

A wandering spirit in this street of tombs,
I sought her yet who still to travel dooms,
From hostel unto hostel o'er the waste,
Her votaries the fitful lamp illumes.

XXX.

But ere the dawn stood trembling at night's gate,
Dark as the night, I reached a portal great,
Wide to the homeless wind, defaced and bare,
While yet it spake of power, and antique state,

XXXI.

Of pillared hall and chambers large and fair,
Which Thought and Art had carven and made rare,
As life by life was laid with stone on stone,
Or flowed through marble veins the beams to bear;

XXXII.

And flowered aloft in capital and frieze,
As roof and wall high rose with years increase;
Withal did slow decay still gild and stain,
Or like a stealthy robber climbed to seize.

6

XXXIII.

Strange lights from windows glared, and stranger sound
Of mingled mourners' grief and revel round—
Sad discords from a world's disorder wrung—
With music broke upon the desert bound.

XXXIV.

A fountain in the forecourt sullen slept,
One wintry tree beside it, wind beswept,
And shorn of its last leaves, which strewed the stone,
Like one above the water, drooped and wept.

XXXV.

And at the threshold, on the shattered stair,
In raiment sad one sate as cloaked in care;
There, too, her sister shape in vernal green,
The lintel old did hang with garlands fair.

XXXVI.

"Who," then I would have cried, "art thou that weep?
And why with mourning festal garlands heap?
Why thus, though kindred, are your hearts in twain!
O Sisters weird this magic house who keep?

XXXVII.

"This magic house, so fair, so disarrayed,
What god, what demon first its foundings laid?
Who thus its treasure to Oblivion casts,
Still hungering at the gate but never stayed?"

XXXVIII.

And I was answered ere my thought found tongue,
As pealing from the gate their voices rung,
Like wailing harp and voice together heard;
With ear intent upon their speech I hung.

7

XXXIX.

" Let no man ask, but he who doth not shrink
To stand at gaze upon thought's giddy brink,
Where breaks the endless sea, and ebbs and flows
The tides of life and death that Time doth drink.

XL.

" Time's very house is this, his daughters we,
Ruin and Renovation, thou dost see,
That sweep or garnish, and its chambers fit
For grief or joy, or whatso guests may be.

XLI.

" Pillared and roofed it is with nights and days,
And windows gemmed in gold, or azure space,
Its table spread, with earth's, for fast or feast,
Between Birth's gate and Death's where all find place.

XLII.

" Close curtained both with mystery and pain,
O'erwrought with costly tears, and heart-hued stain,
And Love the windows dim hath painted o'er
With dreams of dear delight, that wax and wane

XLIII.

" From morn to eve, as through the glowing glass
His vital sun transfigures, as they pass,
Those visionary joys, and hopes, and fears
That mask Life's face—a dream itself, alas !"

XLIV.

But ere they ceased a fairer one forth came,
With cup of welcome and with torch aflame,
In floating raiment soft, and radiant hair,
And thus she sang, each captive sense to claim :—

8

XLV.

"Dream on, O soul, or sleep and take thy rest,
The feast is spread however late the guest;
Let passion drug the cup with secret fire,
Till torturing thought be slain on pleasure's breast.

XLVI.

"Where all are masked thy mask shall be thy face,
Call for the best life gives, and take thy place
At Time's long hostel board; cast off thy care,
And rest you merry in dame Fortune's grace.

XLVII.

"Vex not thy soul until the reckoning day,
Though life be but the least thou hast to pay;
Stand not too late on pleasure's foaming brink,
Nor yet, with sightless eld, outsit the play.

XLVIII.

"Time is thine host, and, ere the day grows old,
To thee his story strange he shall unfold,
Writ in a half-obliterated scroll,
But pictured fair, and graven deep—behold!"

XLIX.

As though a new Pandora raised the lid,
And let life's mystery escape unbid,
Broke sudden on my sight a wonder show,
As through the portal dark I gazed, close hid:

The Sirens Three.

L.

E'en like as one who sits, expectant, dumb,
At gaze before some world's proscenium,
When rolls the curtain from the painted stage,
To see life's play,—Past, Present, and To Come ;

LI.

The drama of the earth before me rolled,
The war of good and evil, new and old,
The fight for very life, for space, for air,
The sum and cost of Being, still untold :

LII.

Since when Time's brooding bird did patient sit
Upon her spherèd egg—the world, to wit,
Potent with life, in ocean, earth, and air,
Ere ever faun or flower did people it.:

LIII.

Since when from countless germs life's tree did grow
From writhing worms about its roots below,
From dragon-shapes that clasp its fossil stem,
To bear love's fruit, and human flowers arow.

LIV.

Where Thought's winged kind among its branches dwell,
Still fertilized by Beauty's potent spell ;
Cast and re-cast in Nature's supple mould,
Through death and change, and birth's transforming cell.

LV.

'Twas pictured here—with boughs outspread thro' space,
Blossomed with stars upon the sky's swart face,
With globing worlds for fruit, that cool or glow
As night and day, like leaves their shadows chase.

LVI.

Out of the dream of ages, sleeping fast,
Out of the dim and unrecorded past,
Out of the caverns of uncounted time,
In life's dark house Man saw the sun at last.

LVII.

Inhuman Man, late come unto the birth,
Wrapped in the swathing bands of mother Earth,
Long his descent, his pedigree obscure,
To his inheritance of strife and dearth.

LVIII.

As from the ground the earth-worm crawls to light,
Speechless and blind, from antenatal night
Man rose on earth, the bitter strife began—
Man rose on earth, and craft did conquer might :

LIX.

Since cruel Nature, careless of her child,
Left him an outcast on the worldly wild,
Cradled in space, and serpent-swathed in time,
And rocked to sleep by death, or dream-beguiled.

LX.

I saw him in his cradle at the first,
With beasts and savage passions, rudely nursed
To snatch uncertain life from Nature's hand,
Niggard or prodigal, through best and worst ;

LXI.

He blindly bore the burden of his day
With his dumb kindred of the primal clay,
Whence drew his blood brute instincts, fiery lusts
That waste his substance still, and tear and slay.

LXII.

A babbling child he sits upon Time's sand,
To the mute sky he cries, he would command ;
Heedless he plays with serpents and with fire,
With life—a toy in his unconscious hand.

LXIII.

Yet hath he held it from that early day,
Though Death did ever plot to snatch away,
And snared his tottering steps with dangers thick,
Prowling in countless shapes beside his way.

LXIV.

Sore was the strife, and little was life's boon
Between the toiling sun and wasting moon,
With lurid pleasures fierce, and horrid rite,
Blind day outworn, the long long sleep won soon.

LXV.

Still Nature, prodigal, did cast his seed
O'er frozen sea, or burning zone, to breed—
Where hand or foot could cling, or heart could beat—
Man's kind on earth, since sprung to flower, or weed.

LXVI.

The rod of Want, the school of bitter Need,
Taught him Life's letters, still so hard to read :
Use gave him skill, and skill new sense to use,
He bent the bow, he bade the ploughshare speed.

LXVII.

Bread for his body and his soul he sought,
Raiment to cloak him from the cold he bought
Of ruthless nature, toiling brain and hand ;
Past all the gates of death his race he brought.

LXVIII.

Lo! infant Thought and Art, Man's children fair
First tottering from the cave, his primal lair;
Babes in the world's wood wandering, to and fro,
To touch man's sordid heart, and lift his care.

LXIX.

Since the first hunter graved his dirk and horn,
Or in the shepherd state was music born—
When Song lay dreaming in the whispering reed,
Ere she discoursed unto the golden morn.

LXX.

Born of life's travail, Virtues, sweet, benign,
Grew like fair daughters of a race divine—
The pillars of Man's house before whose rod
Evil and Good, as twisted snakes, untwine.

LXXI.

But to his roof had fled pale palsied Fear,
The child of Death and Night, but fathered there,
And nursed by Ignorance beside the hearth
To cloud his house with all her mystic gear.

LXXII.

Demon and fetish painted she to scare,
And veils against the light did weave and wear;
Yea, Art and Thought, man's firstlings, fain would bind
From birth to serve her will, her yoke to bear.

LXXIII.

So Man, held hand and foot, a slave behold
Between the soldier-king and priest of old;
By force and fraud bound fast as by two chains—
How long, O Man, how long shall they thee hold?

LXXIV.

" How long ?" again I cried,—but Silence kept
Her finger on the lips of Hope: still slept,
Like clouds upon the mountains, dreams untold,
And Freedom on the tomb of ages wept.

LXXV.

Yet, like a watcher by a beacon fire,
Amid the lurid gloom, and shadows dire,
Wrapped in the cloak of darkness, fold on fold,
I marked through flames portentous shapes aspire.

LXXVI.

Slow streamed the progress vast of human kind,
Out of the primal dark I watched it wind,
Like a full river gleaming towards the sun,
Crested with light, but lost in mists behind.

LXXVII.

I saw the towering crests of ancient state
Arise and pass, and bow themselves to fate:
Captors of men bound still to conquering Time,
And in their triumph drawn to death's dark gate.

14

LXXVIII.

Colossal Egypt on her car rolled by,
Dragged by her crowd of slaves, with lash and cry
Who now, a slave herself, is bought and sold,
And buried in the sand her pride doth lie.

LXXIX.

Athens, supreme with burnished helm and spear,
In art and arms and wisdom shining clear,
To other hands hath passed the lamp of life,
And weep the muses o'er her sculptured bier.

LXXX.

There, clothed as with a robe with power and pride,
Great Rome upon her triumph car did ride
Over the necks of nations and of men,
Unto whose broken wheel still souls are tied.

LXXXI.

All these I saw, as on Time's painted page
The figure of man's life from age to age
Was figured, like his life of years and hours,
And glassed his face—an infant or a mage.

LXXXII.

In boyhood bright beneath the Grecian sun
I saw him stand, intent his race to run—
To touch the golden goal of thought and art,
And daring all man since hath dared or done.

LXXXIII.

The apple of his life to Beauty's hand
Freely he gave, and she so dowered his land,
That still the fond world takes it for her glass,
And gazes, leaving knowledge and command.

15

LXXXIV.

In youth a mystic shadow o'er him fell :
He touched the lover's lute beneath the spell ;
He fought, a knight-at-arms, for lady's grace ;
He prayed a monk austere in haunted cell ;

LXXXV.

Till Nature roused him from his dreams again,
And Reason broke the chains which bound him then ;
New knowledge, power, and beauty filled life's cup,
And rolled the round world to his manhood's ken.

LXXXVI.

Yet old before his time he sits, out-worn
With words and wars, upon the seat of scorn ;
Weary of life's vain round, love's fruitless chase,
False fortune's whirling wheel, fame's empty horn.

LXXXVII.

For here, in living shape and semblance, shone
The passions and the powers man's soul hath won
Through all his ages, like the starry signs
Where through life's year revolves the sleepless sun.

LXXXVIII.

The pattern and the form of thoughts untold ;
The book of being wrought in runes of gold ;
The twisted net that holds all gain and loss
The birth-clothes cover, or the shroud doth fold.

LXXXIX.

The moving tapestry of human date,
Where lives for threads are crossed in love or hate,
Between the narrow beams of dark and day—
Time's shifting loom, the toil of threefold fate.

16

XC.

At their eternal task the sisters dread,
Who spin and weave and shear the slender thread
With all its dyes, that doth sustain and fill
This tangled web from pole to pole outspread.

XCI.

The arras that doth clothe the house of Time,
Stained with the hues of all man's bliss and crime :—
The chequered pageant of the changing earth
Still through its folds doth ever sink and climb :

XCII.

Along the street of days and nights where rolls
The world's car onwards and its throng of souls,
Like captives in a conqueror's triumph chained—
Compelled by fortune's wheel that none controls.

XCIII.

The glittering triumph of youth's golden dreams,
And ardent manhood in the zenith, beams
Of love, and fame, and power that guides the car,
And slow-pulsed eld still warmed in their last gleams.

XCIV.

Masqued with the masquers in that endless race
The hours go by at grief's or passion's pace,
And cloaked alike in poverty or pride,
Through all life's masks Death shows his ashen face

XCV.

The shadow clinging to the feet of life,
As unto day doth cleave his silent wife—
Sower and reaper in the self-same field—
Twin spirits folded in immortal strife.

XCVI.

There good and ill, brothers and bitter foes,
Do strike the balance of man's joys and woes;
And in the traffic of the world's exchange
Oft ill as good, and good as evil goes:

XCVII.

Two knights that battle for Truth's painted targe,
With flashing spears upon Time's river marge,
Where, like the rushing waters, rise their steeds,
And crash together in tremendous charge.

XCVIII.

Their broken harness lies upon Time's plain,
Their wars' receding tide doth cast the slain,
As shifts the battle-ground from age to age,
And earth its grim memorials retain.

XCIX.

These things I marked, as in a moving show
Before mine eyes life passed thro' gloom and glow—
The trappings and the garniture that decked
This house of shadows still from room to room.

C.

Man was; man is; but who shall count the gain,
Or measure out the sum of all life's pain?
So to the play my thought made interlude,
And still to fate's sad music sang refrain.

CI.

Man is, but who can count his being's cost ?
Who metes the water from the pitcher lost ?
The squandered corn upon the sower's path ?
Cast in Time's scale hath good or ill the most ?

CII.

Each out of Babel answers for himself,
As justice he doth love, or gilded pelf :
Who in the school of ignorance should read
Truth's tattered book on thriftless nature's shelf ?

CIII.

Unlettered children, hopeless to the task,
And dumb before life's riddles, still we ask ;
But labour, sole, is answered—patient thought,
And science still doth nature make unmask.

CIV.

Ah ! what is life ?—A coin but stamped and cast
Into Time's treasury counted, weighed, and pass'd,
Staked in the fateful race for weal or woe,
And, gold or silver, changed for lead at last ?

CV.

While dread Necessity, great Nature's nurse,
Who rules man's way for better or for worse,
Still watching by death's bed and birth's doth sit
To pour life's blessing, or to brand its curse.

CVI.

Between the flickering lamps of day and night,
Cloaked in her age-worn mantle care-bedight,
Behold her shape, inexorable, vast—
Blind arbitress o'er changeling wrong and right :

19

CVII.

Who pain, and bliss, and passion, hope, despair,
Casts in life's cup, she, cunning, mixes fair,
And gives, as to a babe, man's helpless lips,
Drawing delicious poison unaware.

CVIII.

Then what is life? Well might we ask again—
A spirit from the cup that fills the brain
With teeming images of love and power,
And high desires 'tis impotent to gain?

CIX.

Protean life which man doth vain pursue
From youth's green meads to age's mountains blue—
The painted fly a breathless child doth chase—
Through all its changing shapes to change but true:

CX.

This quivering bubble, dyed with every stain
Of splendour and of passion, why in vain—
Ah! why?—It sails the summer air—
An iridescent moment lost in rain?

CXI.

But still the cup is passed swift as of yore,
As life each new-come guest doth pledge and pour
The priceless wine into the fragile glass,
Once to the brim filled up, and filled no more.

CXII.

Some drink with eager thirst; some waste their store,
Or drop by drop still watch it shrinking sore;
Some, ere the vital juice hath passed their lips,
The frail cup shatter on the marble floor.

CXIII.

Yet high the feast-tide rolled, and those who fell
Few missed, nor empty long their place did dwell,
For great the press is at earth's table round,
And still new streams that company doth swell.

CXIV.

Ah! bitter was the strife, and hot the breath
Of envy, hate, their smiling masks beneath,
And baleful fires I saw in beauties' eyes,
And rosy ensigns veiled the cheek of death.

CXV.

While grovelled for the crumbs a famished crew,
As starvèd hounds for what men careless threw,
On wastrel bread and refuse fain to feed,
Or none, as deadlier their struggle grew.

CXVI.

For very life at all too dear a cost
As slaves these toiled, while those as counters tost
Their lives for gold, or gold for lives exchanged,
Indifferent, so they did win, who lost.

CXVII.

For those the roses, and for these the rue,
In man's unequal measures paid undue :
Some murmured loud, some patient bore their fate—
The poor were many, and the rich were few.

CXVIII.

Most weary of the sordid throng I grew,
And thence a little space apart withdrew,
Weary of life, that it this thing should be,
Nor other lot for man that hope foreknew.

CXIX.

So to the portal dark I turned again,
And there, as at the first, the Sisters twain—
She who the fruitless garland hung aloft,
She on the shattered stone that wept in vain.

CXX.

But in the forecourt flashed the fountain's stream,
The wintry tree beside its glittering beam
Bore now a cloud of blossom, red and pale,
As if bright spring had touched it in a dream.

CXXI.

Alone I stood in that still house of Time,
All swept and bare it 'was as at the prime,
And but the sea-wind peopled it with sighs,
And, heard afar, the slow waves' rythmic chime.

CXXII.

I saw Time's shape colossal rising stark
Against the endless waves, receding dark
Beneath a rising dawn that never rose
Upon the sea, where yet would Hope embark.

CXXIII.

Yea! Hope arose and drew the painted veil
Of things that are, and furled it like a sail,
And on her gilded prow I stood at gaze
On golden sands beyond the morning pale.

CXXIV.

And from the face of Earth were drawn away,
Like clinging mists that do obscure the day,
The shadows and the fears which have oppressed
Her children long beneath their baneful sway.

CXXV.

As new created in her sculptured sphere,
I saw her rise again translucent, clear,
Robed in the kindling splendour of the sun,
Renascent from the sea of crystal air,

CXXVI.

That limpid broke on her rejoicing shore,
Where life's reviving stream welled evermore
From Nature's fount, through teeming veins that bred
Man's countless kin from one redundant core.

CXXVII.

I saw the dragons slain of lust and greed,
Of gold and power, that waste to serve their need
Poor human lives; and till earth's fruitful fields
With fire and sword, and bloody vengeance breed.

CXXVIII.

No more the nations armed did lie and wait,
Like bandits fierce, to spoil and desolate
What each did hold most dear—no dogs of war
At tyrants' beck, let loose to maim and bait.

CXXIX.

No peoples blind by blinder leaders led
Into the pit of shame, or daily fed
Like swine on empty husks and sophistries,
And frozen custom giving stones for bread.

CXXX.

No selfish castes in internecine strife
Fought like the beasts to win a worthless life ;
No ruthless commerce cheapened hope and health,
Or held to slavish throats starvation's knife.

CXXXI.

No rights usurped, against the common good
Breathed out defiance, and the claims withstood
Of labour and of life, where all by labour lived :
No bonds were there but bonds of brotherhood.

CXXXII.

No temple-gloom obscured the lucent skies,
Nor incense fume of faith's dead sacrifice,
No baneful toil made cities desolate
With hellish smoke at morn and eve to rise.

CXXXIII.

No morbid anchorite with famished creed
Would man persuade to sell his nature's need
Of joy—no fevered dream of future fate
Would snatch life's brimming cup, his human meed.

CXXXIV.

Not there blind dogma flung the bitter fruit
Of discord, burning red, or hate uproot
The flower of innocence, or fraud beguiled,
Or force laid iron hands on man and brute.

CXXXV.

I saw regenerate Man, as stainless, free—
A child again on mother Nature's knee;
His wistful eyes did scan the starry spheres,
His hand outstretched to life's new-flowering tree.

CXXXVI.

The Ages kneeling at his feet did bear
The treasure of their thoughts in caskets rare—
The fire-tried gold of science, and the lore
Of wisdom, bought with costly toil and care.

CXXXVII.

The thoughts each moment from the quivering brain
That spring like flames, or, born with labour pain,
Embodied there I saw—quick thronging spirits fair
From whose inwoven wings light fell like summer rain.

CXXXVIII.

And each in hand did bear the emblems bright
Wherein do art and poesy delight,
And mysteries of science, hid in time,
Her wands of power and globes of knowledge-light.

CXXXIX.

For, more than men, lives Man, through death alive;
Slow moves the progress vast, still cry and strive
New hopes, new thoughts for utterance and for act,
And Use, and Strength, and Beauty yet survive.

CXL.

Yea, beauty's image graven on the mind
Beats with the pulse of life, in life enshrined ;
Irradiant she moves in love's own flame,
And joy with her, and the sweet graces kind.

CXLI.

Like Venus flashing from the lucent sea,
Or, from the earth, the flower Persephone ;
She that was buried, lo! is born again,
And time her resurrection brings to be.

CXLII.

Daughter of earth yet is not mortal she,
Though Time hath shook the blossoms from her tree,
Her spring returns, her summer and her fruit,
And Art by her hath Immortality.

CXLIII.

I saw, I heard no more, for sleep, like rain
Fell soft at last upon my restless brain ;
For Sleep in all the pageant made the last,
And with her poppies swept mine eyes again :

CXLIV.

Yea, far upon her wings then I was borne
All dreamlessly till, like a dream, the morn
Broke on my sense and sight, and, swift and loud,
Day, like a hunter, blew his golden horn.

The
SIRENS·THREE

THE SIRENS THREE

LOST on a sleepless sea, without avail
My soul's ship drifted wide, with idle sail
And slow pulsating oars, that night's blue gulf
Beat noiselessly to Time's recurring tale.

The rolling hours like waves broke, one by one,
Upon the tide of thought time's sands outrun,
And cloudy visions hovered o'er my bed,
Piled to the stars, full soon like cloud undone:

As, like the wan moon through her fleecy sea,
My spirit clove their rack unceasingly,
And struck at last upon an unknown ground,
More still than sleep, more strange than dreamland's be.

IV

THE echoes of lost thoughts wild music made,
Like sirens, heard above the winds that played
Above the rythmic waves tumultous tone,
Upon the hollows of that coast decayed.

V

YEA, on the strand they stood, the Sirens three—
No More, and golden Now, and dark To Be,
Whose vocal harps are love, and hope, and grief;
To these they sang, and waved their hands to me.

VI

WHO thence, unto the shore, escaping, clung,
As from the dread insatiate ocean's tongue
That lapped the barren sand, and evermore,
Above its vain recoil, the Sisters sung.

VII

PRONE on that unknown land, outcast, forlorn,
My soul lay; watching for the eyes of morn;
As from a dying universe adrift,
A naked life—to what dim world new born?

VIII.

All former things had passed, the sea's salt
From Youth's frail ship had washed false hopes
And relics, treasured once, bestrewed the sand,
Wrapped in the clinging weed the seamaid wears.

IX.

The bodies of lost Faith and Love, outcast,
Spurned by the waves, & clinging to the mast,
Were flung upon the shore, mid drift & wreck,—
Time's fragile shells, which frailer lives outlast.

X.

As at the world's end left, the last of men,
Or ere the first was sphered, beyond his ken,
Was I, mid tumbled kosmic fragments cast—
A babe at play within a mammoth's den:

XI.

Mid bones of power extinct, and its lost prey,
With shreds & shards of unknown primal day—
The formless Future, and the Past forgot,
The broken statue, and the sculptor's clay.

XII.

THE blue-breast bird of space his fan outspread
And shook the starry splendour o'er my head—
A wood of eyes that wonder at the world,
Glassed in the world's eyes' wonder, scanned
                                          & read:

XIII.

Each burning orb that did the sky emblaze
Upon my spirit lone cast piercing gaze;
World beyond world enringed, & suns aflame
Shot from night's spangled cloud their storm
                                          of rays.

XIV.

As doth the glass to one bright point intense
Draw the suns' fervour to our shrinking sense;
So, on my soul, the concentrated fire
Of countless suns that moment did
                                          condense.

XV.

My brain, an instant's Atlas, seemed to bear
The Universe immense, & all its' care;
For Thoughts' frail arms intolerable weight,
Since Nature's triumph still is Man's despair.

XVI.

Untilled, unknown, the trackless regions spread
Which Thought, belated wanderer, doth tread,
Where, like river flashing through the night,
The milky way its myriad star-foam shed.

XVII

Cast from what vital source — what teeming brain?
By blind persistent force — from fiery rain —
Suns, moons, & stars, transmuted, globed, & hung,
The dew of Space upon its blue campaign :

XVIII

Trod by the feet of Time, as he doth go,
A labourer night & morn to reap & sow —
Who counts them as they fall, or wonders well
If one should break with all his weight of woe?

XIX.

Each drop a desert, or a battle-ground
Of life in its arena ringed around,
Where without quarter wears the endless war,
Till Death the hunter slips his famished hound.

XX.

Here, circling with the horses of the sun,
Man's fateful race from day to day is run;
Bound in this narrow ring — his crown, his grave,
Still as the world for each is lost or won.

THEN, like a homeless one, my spirit turned
For shelter 'neath the roofless void, &, spurned
From the star-desert to the stoney one,
Scanned the dark waste where yet no hearth fire
burned:

But through the veil of night, around me there,
Rose towering shapes clothed in the voiceless air,
Like kings enthroned amid their powers' decay —
Statue, & ruined shrine, & temple bare:

Dolmen, & sphinx, & Greek or Gothic fane,
The shattered caskets of man's winged brain,
Whose flight hath left them empty, desolate,
Sublime in ruin on the crumbling plain.

The perished bodies frail that once did house
His restless soul, & heard his sacred vows
To his own likeness, dressed in speech or stone,
Ere he foreswore them for some fairer spouse.

XXV
He sought for Truth, & cried "where dost thou dwell?"
Ten thousand tongues replied, but none could tell:
They held their peace, & then the stones did cry—
"Lo! Truth sits naked by the wayside well."

XXVI.
She sitteth naked since they drove her out
From Babel of the Creeds to wastes of Doubt;
There hath she wandered long in dens & caves,
Through Custom's winter, & through Reason's
drought.

XXVII.
They would have cloaked her as a shameful thing;
Force brought her chains, & Fraud a marriage ring,
But Truth, afrighted, fled the market place
Where lies were coined in gold, & Craft was king.

XXVIII.
And still she flies from sacred fount, & school,
When man defiles, or doth his kind befool;
And still they wait, the halt, the lame, the blind,
Though Truth, the angel, troubleth not the pool.

XXIX

wandering spirit in this street of tombs,
I sought her yet who still to travel dooms,
From hostel unto hostel o'er the waste,
Her votaries the fitful lamp illumes

XXX

But ere the dawn stood trembling at night's gate,
Dark as the night. I reached a portal great,
Wide to the homeless wind, defaced & bare,
While yet it spake of power, & antique state,

XXXI

Of pillared hall & chambers large & fair,
Which Thought & Art had carven & made rare,
As life by life was laid with stone on stone,
Or flowed through marble veins the beams to bear;

XXXII

And flowered aloft in capital & frieze,
As roof and wall high rose with years increase;
Withal did slow decay still gild & stain,
Or like a stealthy robber climbed to sieze.

[sound

STRANGE lights from windows glared, & stranger
Of mingled mourners grief & revel round –
Sad discords from a world's disorder wrung –
With music broke upon the desert bound.

XXXIV

A fountain in the forecourt sullen slept,
One wintry tree beside it, wind beswept,
And shorn of its last leaves, which strewed the
stone,
Like one above the water, drooped & wept.

XXXV

And at the threshold, on the shattered stair,
In raiment sad one sate as cloaked in care;
There, too, her sister shape in vernal green,
The lintel old did hang with garlands fair.

XXXVJ.

"Who", then I would have cried, "art thou that weep?"
"And why with mourning festal garlands heap?
Why thus, though kindred, are your hearts in twain!
O Sisters wierd this magic house who keep?"

xxxvij

This magic house, so fair, so disarrayed,
What god, what demon first its foundings
                                    laid?
Who thus its treasure to Oblivion casts,
Still hungering at the gate but never stayed?"

xxxviij

And I was answered ere my thought found tongue,
As pealing from the gate their voices rung,
Like wailing harp & voice together heard:
With ear intent upon their speech I hung.

xxx
ix.

"Let no man ask, but he who doth not shrink
To stand at gaze upon thought's giddy brink,
Where breaks the endless sea, & ebbs & flows
The tides of life & death that Time doth drink."

XL.

TIME'S very house is this, his daughters we,
Ruin & Renovation thou dost see,
That sweep or garnish, & its chambers fit
For grief or joy, or whatso guests may be.

XLI

Pillared & roofed it is with nights & days,
And windows gemmed in gold, or azure space,
Its table spread, with earth's, for fast or feast,
Between Birth's gate & Death's where all find place.

XLII.

Close curtained both with mystery & pain,
O'erwrought with costly tears, & heart-hued stain,
And Love the windows dim hath painted o'er
With dreams of dear delight, that wax & wane

XLIII.

From morn to eve, as through the glowing glass
His vital sun transfigures, as they pass,
Those visionary joys, & hopes, & fears
That mask Life's face — a dream itself, alas! "

XLIV.

BUT ere they ceased a fairer one forth came,
With cup of welcome & with torch aflame,
In floating raiment soft, & radiant hair,
And thus she sang, each captive sense to claim:-

XLV.

"Dream on, O soul, or sleep & take thy rest,
The feast is spread however late the guest;
Let passion drug the cup with secret fire,
Till torturing thought be slain on pleasure's breast.

XLVI.

Where all are masked thy mask shall be thy face,
Call for the best life gives, & take thy place
At Time's long hostel board; cast off thy care,
And rest you merry in dame Fortune's grace.

XLVII.

Vex not thy soul until the reckoning day,
Though life be but the least thou hast to pay;
Stand not too late on pleasure's foaming brink,
Nor yet, with sightless eld, outsit the play.

XLVIII

Time is thine host, &, ere the day grows old,
To thee his story strange he shall unfold,
Writ in a half-obliterated scroll,
But pictured fair, & graven deep - behold!

XLIX

As though a new Pandora raised the lid,
And let life's mystery escape unbid,
Broke sudden on my sight a wonder show,
As through the portal dark I gazed, close hid;

L.

E'en like as one who sits, expectant, dumb,
At gaze before some world's proscenium,
When rolls the curtain from the painted stage,
To see life's play – Past, Present, & To Come;

LI

The drama of the earth before me rolled,
The war of good & evil, new & old,
The fight for very life, for space, for air,
The sum & cost of Being, still untold.

LII.

SINCE, when Time's brooding bird did patient sit
Upon her spheréd egg, the world. To wit,
Potent with life, in ocean, earth, & air,
Ere ever faun or flower did people it:

LIII.

Since when from countless germs life's tree did grow
From writhing worms about its roots below,
From dragon-shapes that clasp its fossil stem,
To bear love's fruit, & human flowers arow.

LIV.

Where Thoughts' winged kind among its branches [dwell,
Still fertilized by Beauty's potent spell;
Cast & re-cast in Nature's supple mould,
Through death & change, & birth's transforming cell.

LV.

'Twas pictured here — with boughs outspread thro' [space,
Blossomed with stars upon the sky's swart face,
With globing worlds for fruit, that cool or glow
As night & day, like leaves their shadows chase.

LVI

OUT of the dream of ages, sleeping fast,
Out of the dim & unrecorded past,
Out of the caverns of uncounted time,
In life's dark house Man saw the sun at last.

LVII

Inhuman Man, late come unto the birth,
Wrapped in the swathing bands of mother Earth,
Long his descent, his pedigree obscure,
To his inheritance of strife & dearth.

LVIII

As from the ground the earth-worm crawls to light,
Speechless & blind, from antenatal night
Man rose on earth, the bitter strife began —
Man rose on earth, & craft did conquer might:

LIX.

Since cruel Nature, careless of her child,
Left him an outcast on the worldly wild,
Cradled in space & serpent-swathed in time,
And rocked to sleep by death, or dream beguiled.

LX.

I SAW him in his cradle at the first,
With beasts & savage passions, rudely nursed
To snatch uncertain life from Nature's hand,
Niggard or prodigal, through best & worst;

LXI.

He blindly bore the burden of his day
With his dumb kindred of the primal clay,
Whence drew his blood brute instincts, fiery lusts
That waste his substance still, & tear & slay.

LXII

A babbling child he sits upon Time's sand,
To the mute sky he cries, he would command;
Heedless he plays with serpents & with fire,
With life-a toy in his unconscious hand.

LXIIJ

YET hath he held it from that early day,
Though Death did ever plot to snatch away,
And snared his tottering steps with dangers thick,
Prowling in countless shapes beside his way.

LXIV.

Sore was the strife, & little was life's boon
Between the toiling sun & wasting moon,
With lurid pleasures fierce, & horrid rite,
Blind day outworn, The long long sleep won
                                                           soon.

LXV

Still Nature, prodigal, did cast his seed
O'er frozen sea, or burning zone, to breed—
Where hand or foot could cling, or heart could beat
Man's kind on earth, since sprung to flower, or
                                         weed.

LXVI.

HE rod of Want, the school of bitter Need
  Taught him Life's letters, still so hard to read:
  Use gave him skill, & skill new sense to use;
  He bent the bow, he bade the ploughshare speed.

LXVIJ.

Bread for his body & his soul he sought,
  Raiment to cloak him from the cold he bought
  Of ruthless nature, toiling brain & hand;
  Past all the gates of death his race he brought.

LXVIIJ.

LO! infant Thought & Art, Man's children fair
  First tottering from the cave, his primal lair;
  Babes in the world's wood wandering, to & fro,
  To touch man's sordid heart, & lift his care,

LXIX.

Since the first hunter graved his dirk & horn,
  Or in the shepherd state was music born —
  When Song lay dreaming in the whispering reed,
  Ere she discoursed unto the golden morn.

LXX

BORN of life's travail, Virtues, sweet, benign,
Grew like fair daughters of a race divine,
The pillars of Man's house before whose rod
Evil & Good, as twisted snakes, untwine.

LXXI.

But to his roof had fled pale palsied Fear,
The child of Death & Night, but fathered there,
And nursed by Ignorance beside the hearth
To cloud his house with all her mystic gear.

LXXII.

Demon & fetish painted she to scare,
And veils against the light did weave & wear;
Yea, Art & Thought, man's firstlings, fain would bind
From birth to serve her will, her yoke to bear.

LXXIII.

O Man, held hand & foot, a slave behold
Between the soldier-king & priest of old;
By force & fraud bound fast as by two chains—
How long, O Man, how long shall they thee hold?

LXXIV.

"How long?" Again, I cried,—
but Silence kept
Her finger on the lips of Hope: still slept,
Like clouds upon the mountains, dreams
untold,
And Freedom on the tomb of ages wept.

LXXV.

Yet, like a watcher by a beacon fire,
Amid the lurid gloom of shadows dire,
Wrapped in the cloak of darkness, fold on
fold,
I marked through flames
portentous shapes
aspire.

LXXVI.

SLOW streamed the progress vast of humankind,
Out of the primal dark I watched it wind,
Like a full river gleaming towards the sun,
Crested with light, but lost in mists behind.

LXXVII.

I saw the towering crests of ancient state
Arise & pass, & bow themselves to fate:
Captors of men bound still to conquering Time,
And in their triumph drawn to death's dark gate.

LXXVIII.

Colossal Egypt on her car rolled by,   I'd cry;
Dragged by her crowd of slaves, with lash
Who now, a slave herself, is bought & sold,
And buried in the sand her pride doth lie.

LXXIX.

Athens, supreme with burnished helm & spear,
In art & arms & wisdom shining clear,
To other hands hath passed the lamp of life,
And weep the muses o'er her sculptured bier.

LXXX.

There, clothed as with a robe with power & [pride,
Great Rome upon her triumph car did ride
Over the necks of nations & of men,
Unto whose broken wheel still souls are
                                        tied.

LXXXI

ALL these I saw, as on time's painted page
The figure of man's life from age to age
Was figured like his life of years & hours,
And glassed his face—an infant or a mage.

LXXXII

In boyhood bright beneath the Grecian sun,
I saw him stand, intent his race to run—
To touch the golden goal of thought & art,
And daring all man since hath dared or done.

LXXXIII

The apple of his life to Beauty's hand
Freely he gave, & she so dowered his land,
That still tha fond world takes it for her glass,
And gazes, leaving knowledge & command.

In youth a mystic shadow o'er him fell:
He touched the lover's lute beneath the spell;
He fought, a knight-at-arms, for lady's grace,
He prayed a monk austere in haunted cell.

Till Nature roused him from his dreams again,
And Reason broke the chains which bound him then;
New knowledge, power, & beauty filled life's cup,
And rolled the round world to his manhood's ken.

Yet old before his time he sits, outworn,
With words of wars upon the seat of scorn;
Weary of life's vain round, love's fruitless chase,
False fortune's whirling wheel, fame's empty horn.

For here, in living shape of semblance, shone
The passions of the powers man's soul hath won
Through all his ages, like the starry signs
Where through life's year revolves the sleepless
sun.

LXXXVIII

The pattern & the form of thoughts untold;
The book of being wrought in runes of gold;
The twisted net that holds all gain & loss
The birth-clothes cover, or the shroud doth fold.

LXXXIX.

The moving tapestry of human date,
Where lives for threads are crossed in love or hate
Between the narrow beams of dark & day —
Time's shifting loom, the toil of threefold fate.

XC.

At their eternal task the sisters dread,
Who spin & weave & shear the slender thread
With all its dyes, that doth sustain & fill
This tangled web from pole to pole outspread.

XCI.

The arras that doth clothe the house of Time,
Stained with the hues of all man's bliss & crime:—
The chequered pageant of the changing earth
Still through its folds doth ever sink
      & climb:

Along the street of days & nights where rolls
The world's car onwards & its throng of souls,
Like captives in a conquerors' triumph chained –
Compelled by fortune's wheel that none controuls.

XCIII.

The glittering triumph of youth's golden dreams,
And ardent manhood in the zenith beams
Of love, & fame, & power that guides the car,
And slow-pulsed eld still warmed in their last gleams

XCIV.

Masked with the masquers in that endless race
The hours go by at grief's or passion's pace,
And cloaked alike in poverty or pride,
Through all life's masks death shows his ashen face.

XCV.

– The shadow clinging to the feet of life,
As unto day doth cleave his silent wife –
Sower & reaper in the self same field –
Twin spirits folded in immortal strife.

XCVI.

THERE good & ill, brothers & bitter foes,
Do strike the balance of man's joys & woes;
And in the traffic of the world's exchange
Oft ill as good, & good as evil goes:

XCVII

Two knights that battle for Truth's painted targe,
With flashing spears upon Time's river marge,
Where, like the rushing waters, rise their steeds,
And crash together in tremendous charge

XCVIII

Their broken harness lies upon time's plain,
Their wars' receding tide doth cast the slain,
As shifts the battle ground from age to age,
And earth its grim memorials retain

XCIX.

These things I marked, as in a moving show
Before mine eyes life passed thro' gloom & glow.
The trappings & the garniture that decked
This house of shadows still from room to room

C.

MAN was; man is; but who shall count the
Or measure out the sum of all life's pain?
So to the play my thought made interlude,
And still to fates' sad music sang refrain.

CI.

Man is, but who can count his being's cost?
Who metes the water from the pitcher lost?
The squandered corn upon the sower's path?
Cast in time's scale hath good or ill the most?

CII.

Each out of Babel answers for himself,
As justice he doth love, or gilded pelf:
Who in the school of ignorance should read
Truth's tattered book on thriftless nature's shelf?

CIII.

Unlettered children, hopeless to the task,
And dumb before life's riddles, still we ask;
But labour, sole, is answered - patient thought,
And science still doth nature make unmask.

CIV.

Ah! what is life? - A coin but stamped & cast
Into time's treasury counted, weighed, & pass'd,
Staked in the fateful race for weal or woe,
And, gold or silver, changed for lead at last?

CV.

WHILE dread Necessity, great Nature's nurse,
Who rules man's way for better or for worse,
Still watching by death's bed & birth's doth sit
To pour life's blessing, or to brand its curse.

CVI.

Between the flickering lamps of day & night,
Cloaked in her age-worn mantle care-bedight,
Behold her shape, inexorable, vast —
Blind arbitress o'er changeling wrong & right:

CVII.

Who pain, & bliss, & passion, hope, despair,
Casts in life's cup, she, cunning, mixes fair,
And gives, as to a babe, man's helpless lips,
Drawing delicious poison unaware.

CVIII.

Then what is life? Well might we ask again —
A spirit from the cup that fills the brain
With teeming images of love & power,
And high desires 'tis impotent to gain?

CIX.

PROTEAN life which man doth vain pursue
From youth's green meads to ages' mountain's blue
The painted fly a breathless child doth chase—
Through all its changing shapes to change but true.

CX.

This quivering bubble, dyed with every stain
Of splendour & of passion, why in vain—
Ah! why?—It sails the summer air—
An iridescent moment lost in rain?

CXI

BUT still the cup is passed swift as of yore,
As life each new come guest doth pledge & pour
The priceless wine into the fragile glass,
Once to the brim filled up, & filled no more.

CXII.

Some drink with eager thirst; some waste their store,
Or drop by drop still watch it shrinking sore;
Some, ere the vital juice hath passed their lips,
The frail cup shatter on the marble floor.

CXIII.

Yet high the feast-tide rolled, & those who fell
Few missed, nor empty long their place did dwell,
For great the press is at earth's table round,
And still new streams that company doth swell.

CXIV.

Ah! bitter was the strife, & hot the breath
Of envy, hate, their smiling masks beneath,
And baleful fires I saw in beauties' eyes,
And rosy ensigns veiled the cheek of death.

CXV.

WHILE grovelled for the crumbs a famished crew,
As starved hounds for what men careless
On wastrel bread & refuse fain to feed,
Or none, as deadlier their struggle grew.

CXVI.

For very life at all too dear a cost
As slaves these toiled, while those as counters tost
Their lives for gold, or gold for lives exchanged,
Indifferent, so they did win, who lost.

CXVII.

For those the roses, & for these the rue,
In man's unequal measure paid undue:
Some murmured loud, some patient bore their fate_
The poor were many, & the rich were few.

CXVIII.

MOST weary of the sordid throng I grew,
And thence a little space apart withdrew;
Weary of life, that it this thing should be,
Nor other lot for man that hope foreknew.

CXIX.

So to the portal dark I turned again,
And there, as at the first, the Sisters twain—
She who the fruitless garland hung aloft,
She on the shattered stone that wept in vain.

CXX.

But in the forecourt flashed the fountain's stream,
The wintry tree beside its glittering beam
Bore now a cloud of blossom, red & pale,
As if bright Spring had touched it in a
dream.

CXXI.

ALONE I stood in that still house of Time,
All swept & bare it was as at the prime,
  And but the sea-wind peopled it with sighs,
And, heard afar, the slow wave's rythmic chime.

CXXII.

I saw Time's shape colossal rising stark
Against the endless waves; receding dark
Beneath a rising dawn that never rose
Upon the sea, where yet would Hope embark

CXXIII.

Yea! Hope arose & drew the painted veil
Of things that are, & furled it like a sail,
And on her gilded prow I stood at gaze
On golden sands beyond the morning pale

CXXIV.

AND from the face of Earth
were drawn away,
Like clinging mists that do obscure the day,
The shadows of the fears which have oppressed
Her children long beneath their baneful sway.

CXXV.

As new created in her sculptured sphere,
I saw her rise again translucent, clear,
Robed in the kindling splendour of the sun,
Renascent from the sea of crystal air,

CXXVI.

That limpid broke on her rejoicing shore,
Where life's reviving stream welled evermore
From Nature's fount, through teeming veins that
Man's countless kin from one redundant bred
core.

CXXVII.

I SAW the dragons slain of lust & greed
Of gold & power, that waste to serve their need
Poor human lives; & till earth's fruitful fields
With fire & sword, & bloody vengeance breed.

CXXVIII.

No more the nations armed did lie in wait,
Like bandits fierce, to spoil & desolate
What each did hold most dear — no dogs of war
At tyrants' beck, let loose to maim & bait.

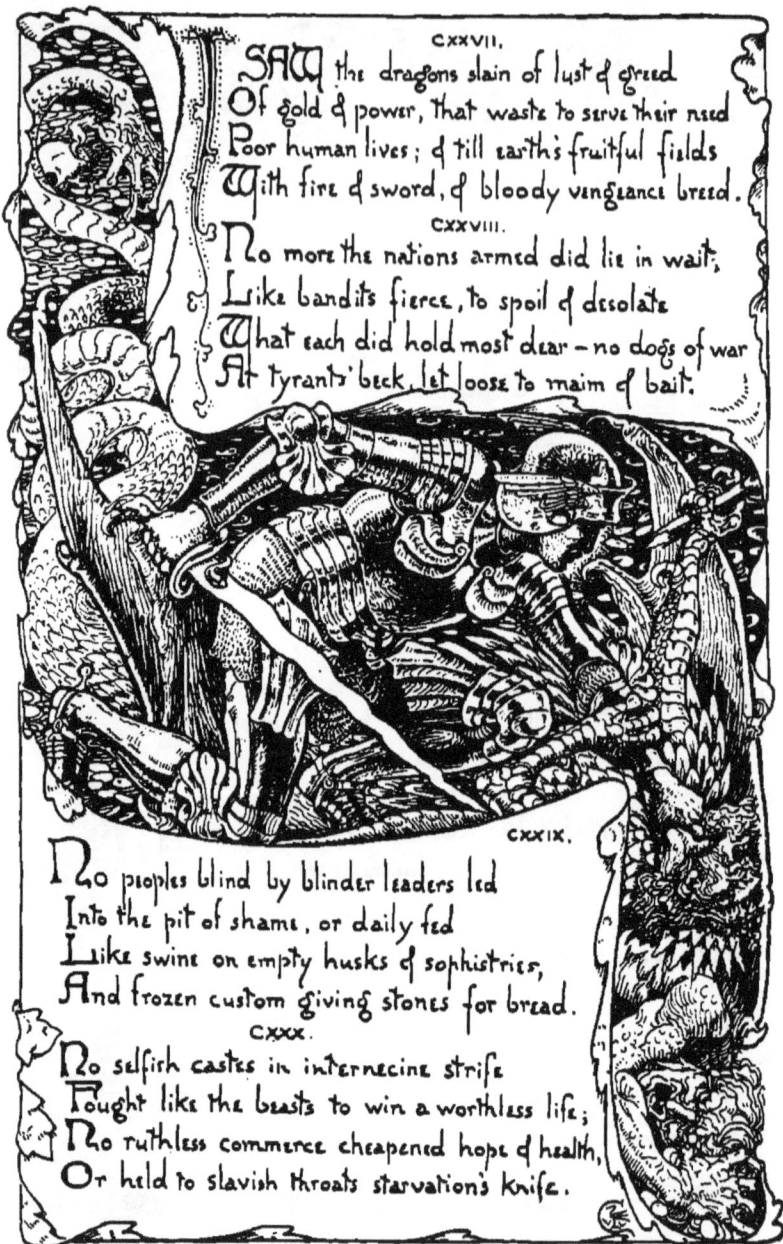

CXXIX.

No peoples blind by blinder leaders led
Into the pit of shame, or daily fed
Like swine on empty husks of sophistries,
And frozen custom giving stones for bread.

CXXX.

No selfish castes in internecine strife
Fought like the beasts to win a worthless life;
No ruthless commerce cheapened hope & health,
Or held to slavish throats starvation's knife.

CXXXI.

No rights usurped, against the common good
Breathed out defiance, & the claims withstood
Of labour & of life, where all by labour lived:
No bonds were there but bonds of brotherhood.

CXXXII.

No temple-gloom obscured the lucent skies,
Nor incense fume of faiths dead sacrifice,
No baneful toil made cities desolate
With hellish smoke at morn & eve to rise.

CXXXIII.

No morbid anchorite with famished creed
Would man persuade to sell his natures need
Of joy — no fevered dream of future fate
Would snatch life's brimming cup, his human meed.

CXXXIV.

Not there blind dogma flung the bitter fruit
Of discord, burning red, or hate uproot
The flower of innocence, or fraud beguiled,
Or force laid iron hands on man & brute.

CXXXV

I SAW regenerate Man, as stainless, free_
A child again on mother Nature's knee;
His wistful eyes did scan the starry spheres,
His hand outstretched to life's new-flowering tree.

CXXXVI

The Ages kneeling at his feet did bear
The treasure of their thoughts in caskets rare_
The fire-tried gold of science, & the lore
Of wisdom, bought with costly toil & care.

CXXXVII   [brain

The thoughts, each moment from the quivering
That spring like flames, or, born with labour pain,
Embodied there I saw,—quick thronging spirits fair
From whose inwoven wings light fell like summer rain.

CXXXVIII

And each in hand did bear the emblems bright
Wherein do art & poesy delight,
And mysteries of science, hid in Time,
Her wands of power & globes of knowledge-light.

CXXXIX   [death alive

FOR, more than men, lives Man, through
  Slow moves the progress vast, still cry of strive
New hopes, new thoughts for utterance & for act,
And Use, of Strength, of Beauty yet survive.

CXL
Yea beauty's image graven on the mind
  Beats with the pulse of life, in life enshrined;
Irradiant she moves in love's own flame,
And joy with her, of the sweet graces kind.

CXLI
Like Venus flashing from the lucent sea,
Or, from the earth, the flower Persephone;
She that was buried, lo! is born again,
And time her resurrection brings to be.

CXLII
Daughter of earth yet is not mortal she,
Though hath shook the blossoms from her tree,
Her spring returns, her summer & her fruit,
  And Art by her hath
     Immortality.

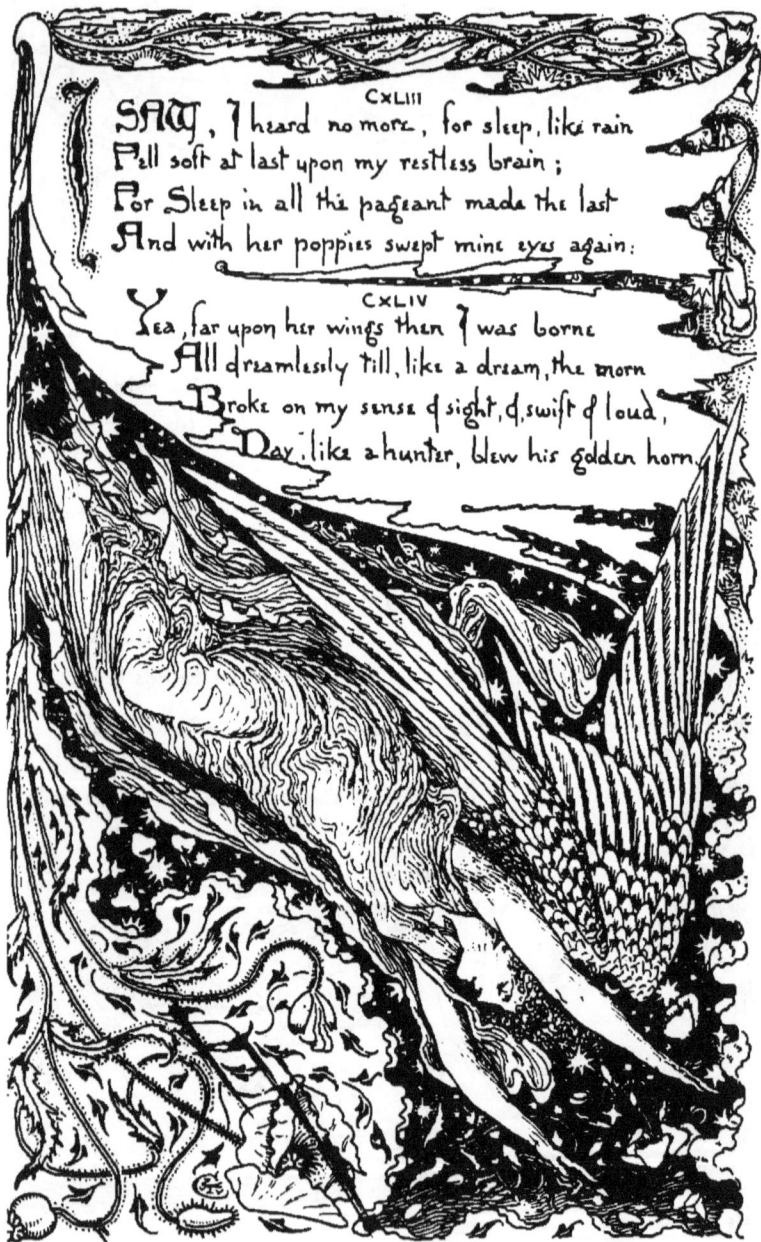

CXLIII

SAW, I heard no more, for sleep, like rain
Fell soft at last upon my restless brain;
For Sleep in all the pageant made the last
And with her poppies swept mine eyes again:

CXLIV

Yea, far upon her wings then I was borne
All dreamlessly till, like a dream, the morn
Broke on my sense of sight, & swift & loud,
Day, like a hunter, blew his golden horn.